EXTINCT

IN THIS SERIES BY BEN GARROD AND GABRIEL UGUETO

Hallucigenia

Dunkleosteus

Trilobite

Lisowicia

Tyrannosaurus rex

Megalodon

Thylacine

Hainan gibbon

ALSO BY BEN GARROD

The Chimpanzee and Me

So You Think You Know About Dinosaurs? series:

Diplodocus

Triceratops

Spinosaurus

Tyrannosaurus rex

Stegosaurus

Velociraptor

EXTINCT
DUNKLEOSTEUS

Ben Garrod

Illustrated by Gabriel Ugueto

ZEPHYR

An imprint of Head of Zeus

This is a Zephyr book, first published in the UK in 2021
by Head of Zeus Ltd
This paperback edition first published in the UK in 2022
by Head of Zeus Ltd, part of Bloomsbury Publishing Plc

9 7 5 3 1 2 4 6 8

A catalogue record for this book is available from
the British Library.

ISBN (PB): 9781838935306
ISBN (E): 9781838935313

Typesetting and design
by Catherine Gaffney

Printed and bound in Serbia
by Publikum d.o.o.

Head of Zeus Ltd
5–8 Hardwick Street
London EC1R 4RG

WWW.HEADOFZEUS.COM

'No water, no life. No blue, no green.'

Dr Sylvia Earle

CONTENTS

INTRODUCTION

For as long as there has been life on Earth, there has been extinction, and given enough time, all species will one day go extinct. It is all too easy to think extinction is terrible and that we should do all we can to stop a species from going extinct. That makes complete sense, doesn't it? The loss of a species seems an awful and unnatural process, caused by the effects of humans, right?

The concept of extinction is something many of us are familiar with but, in fact, it's one we might not fully understand. Very often, extinction is a sad, unacceptable and disastrous ending for a species, but from the point of view of a biologist, it is a fundamental part of nature and is as important to a species as moving, feeding and breeding.

I'm an evolutionary biologist and I've worked with some of the strangest, most beautiful, iconic and heartbreakingly threatened animals on our planet. I understand how species go extinct and why. But it is still a deeply upsetting event for me when I hear a species (any species) has gone extinct – or worse, is rapidly being pushed into the history books because of us. We are bombarded by endless news reports about species threatened with extinction, habitats being destroyed and the impacts of global climate change.

I wanted to write this series to explain what's at stake if we carry on as we are. I want to explore extinction as a biological process and investigate why it can sometimes be a positive thing for evolution, as well as, at times, the most destructive force in nature. Let's put it under the microscope and find out everything there is to know about it. Extinction is an incredible process and understanding it enables us to understand the world that little bit better and to make a difference.

When a species is declared extinct, we place a dagger symbol (†) next to its name when it's listed or mentioned in a scientific manner. So, if you do see the name of a species with a little dagger after it, you'll know why. It's extinct.

In this series, I have written about eight fantastic species. Starting with *Hallucigenia* (†), then *Dunkleosteus* (†) and trilobites (†), through to *Lisowicia* (†), *Tyrannosaurus rex* (†) and megalodon (†), before finishing on the thylacine (†) and lastly, the Hainan gibbon. Of these, only the Hainan gibbon does not have a dagger next to its scientific name, meaning it is the only one we still have a chance of saving.

Professor Ben Garrod

WHAT IS EXTINCTION?

SPECIES EVOLVE; they adapt and change to their environments and eventually, they go extinct. But don't get me wrong. Just because extinction is natural, it does not mean we should sit back and let it happen. Getting burned by the sun is natural but we still sensibly put on sun lotion to protect ourselves. Each extinction is different, each loss unique, and the truth is that while sometimes we can't do anything to tackle extinction, there are times when we can.

Before investigating when we should try to tackle extinction, we first need to understand it as a natural process. What drives extinction, and what makes some species go extinct more easily than others? When we hear the words 'extinct' or 'extinction', we usually think two things. First, we imagine the dinosaurs, because they're probably the most iconic and familiar group to go through the extinction process. I bet you thought of a *Tyrannosaurus rex*, *Diplodocus* or *Triceratops*, didn't you? Second, we often think that if something has gone extinct then maybe it was a bit rubbish in some way and, possibly, even deserved to disappear.

Well, both ideas are wrong. First, the dinosaurs are most certainly not the only group to have faced extinction, and, as I am sure many of you know, they technically never actually completely died out, but that's a story for another time. And second, as I've already mentioned, going extinct is natural and happens to pretty much every kind of animal, plant, fungi, bacteria and other type of life form that has ever existed or is ever likely to, and has nothing to do with how 'good' or 'bad' a species is.

Even a quick look at extinction shows us how widespread, devastating and yet important it is. But before we understand all that, what exactly do we mean by the word extinct? We may have a general idea that it's something to do with a species not being 'alive' anymore. Something is extinct when the last individual of that species or group dies and there are absolutely no more to replace it. Because extinction has been present since the very first life on Earth popped into existence, this must mean that loads and loads of species have gone extinct.

It's difficult to get your head around how many species have already gone extinct. Scientists predict that as many as 99 per cent of the species that have ever lived are extinct. If you're wondering how many species that might actually be, then if their calculations are correct, it means we have already lost an almost unbelievable five billion species from our planet.

It's hard to be certain because many of these extinctions stretch back millions (or even hundreds of millions) of years and because there wasn't a scientist standing there with a camera or a notebook, we shall never know about many of these species. Even today, scientists believe that there may be 10–14 million different species (although some scientists believe this figure might even be as high as one trillion), but of those, only 1.2 million have been documented and recorded in a proper scientific way, meaning we don't know about 90 per cent of life on planet Earth right now.

Here's where it gets a little complicated. Extinction is natural. Even we human beings will go extinct one day. It might sound sad but that's because you're thinking from the point of view of a person. We are simply one of those

14 million or so species, remember. Usually, a species has about 10 million years or so of evolving, eating, chasing, playing, maybe doing homework, building nests or even going to the moon before it goes extinct and ends up in the history (or even prehistory) books. Some species last longer than this, some are around for less time.

Every single species evolves to be perfectly suited to a particular ecosystem or habitat and acts in a way that will help it survive and have young. We call this its niche. Extinction happens when a species can no longer survive in its niche. Lots of different things can cause this and some are more natural than others. Some kill off one species and others cause the loss of thousands or even millions of species at once, making extinction one of the most complex, interesting and important things to study in science.

WHY DO SPECIES GO EXTINCT?

A RECENT report stated that approximately one million (1,000,000) species on Earth are threatened with extinction. This number already sounds unthinkably high, but it only includes animals and plants and not any of the other groups of living organisms essential to the well-being of the planet. If they were included, then the number would be even higher. Much higher.

But why *do* species go extinct? It's not as though human hunters will kill all these species and realistically, climate change can't be responsible for every single loss. As you'll see, there are lots of reasons for extinction, but is there a common link? What makes certain species more likely to go extinct than others? It's an interesting question, which many scientists are investigating.

At its most simple, extinction happens when something bad happens too quickly in the environment of a species or is too severe for the species to overcome. Imagine if a small population of frogs lived on a tiny island and on that island, a volcano erupted, covering the island with lava. If the eruption was sudden and the frogs had nowhere to go... well then, it's bye-bye frogs. But what if the eruption happened more slowly and the frogs had time to escape? Maybe some find a safe, damp rock ledge or a tiny stream that survived the lava flow? It's possible that one or two could survive and the species might just make it. Hurray!

When a species does not have the opportunity to respond to a change in the environment, then it is likely to go extinct. What sort of response from the species do we mean here? Well, it might be a physical change, such as colour or size, or a change in behaviour, such as moving to another habitat or eating something different. It might also be a change so small it's only seen right down in its genes, in the DNA. In terms of what sort of 'changes in the environment' might cause an extinction, these can be either in the physical environment of the species, such as habitat destruction in the forests of Borneo, higher temperatures in the Arctic, or increased acidic conditions on the Great Barrier Reef. Or maybe in its 'biological environment', such as the arrival of a new predator, like cane toads being introduced to Australia. Or it might be the development of a new deadly disease – for example, a virus which might start in bats, jumping to humans and then to great apes in the wild. For each of these changes, the species needs to adapt, or it will die.

Scientists have estimated that the average 'lifespan' of a species is between one million and 10 million years, before it goes extinct. Let's look more closely at the variety of causes that can contribute directly or indirectly to the extinction of a species, or group of species.

DISEASES, PREDATION AND COMPETITION

You might wonder how a disease can be down to humans, but if we take a particularly horrible measles-like condition called canine distemper virus, it shows us how the influence of humans can lead a disease to have a catastrophic effect on wildlife. Canine distemper virus (or CDV) was found in dogs and didn't pose a problem for other species. Then, in 1994, scientists discovered that CDV had jumped from dogs to cats, but not just any cats. In East Africa, in the Serengeti National Park, many lions were becoming sick and no one really knew why.

It was eventually found that they were suffering from CDV, but it was too late to save them and around 30 per cent of the lions there died. It is thought lions and dogs may have fed at the same kills, or even that lions killed and ate the dogs. Whatever happened, it was humans who introduced dogs into the area, and then nature did what it does best: it allowed an organism (in this case the virus) to evolve, change and adapt, and in this instance, it found a new species to act as its host.

Predation is another factor which may lead to extinction. One very interesting example is the Jamaican giant galliwasp, a 30cm-long shiny lizard. This species is probably now extinct because people intentionally introduced mongooses from India to eat the rats they had accidentally introduced across the Caribbean. But instead of eating the rats (which were also predators), the mongooses ate the galliwasps. None have been seen since 1840, so sadly, they are more than likely extinct, because humans introduced a predator to kill another predator.

Introduced predators can have a devastating impact on island ecosystems. In the Caribbean, Javan mongooses preyed on native wildlife, such as the strangely named galliwasps.

COEXTINCTION

Not every species gets on, but sometimes the existence of one species depends on another. If one dies out, then it means certain death for the other. When this happens, we call it coextinction. A famous example was seen in New Zealand, with the moa. These were huge birds, as much as 230kg in weight and 3.6m in height. When humans hunted the flightless moa into extinction, their main predator, the Haast's eagle, lost its food source, and not long after the moa died out, the Haast's eagle did too.

GENETIC MIXING

This isn't pollution in the way you might normally understand it, but every species has a set of genetic data unique to that particular group. It's like the recipe for that species. If any little bit of it is changed, then it becomes a different species. When the genetic material for a species is altered by the presence of 'other' genetic material, we call this 'genetic mixing'. This can happen naturally, or because humans are to blame.

As well as occurring between species, genetic pollution can occur within a species. In northeastern Canada, millions of Atlantic salmon are farmed in huge meshed enclosures. They're meant to be kept separately from the wild Atlantic salmon, but storms allow these farmed fish to escape and breed with the wild ones. Wild salmon have millions of years of evolution, which has given them the best opportunity to survive, but farmed fish are specially bred to have different qualities, such as growing quickly and putting on weight. When they bred with the wild salmon, their offspring were much less efficient at surviving in the wild. The influence of these farmed fish escapees has the potential to change the success of the entire species.

HABITAT DESTRUCTION

It is clear to see how habitat destruction and change is causing extinctions now. We only have to look at the forests being torn down in Indonesia, Malaysia and West Africa to clear land for palm oil production, or the Great Barrier Reef where the dumping of chemicals and other waste products is polluting and killing the reef. Habitat destruction has always featured significantly as a cause of extinctions throughout the history of life on Earth.

Even the world in which the subject of this book, *Dunkleosteus*, evolved, meaning the habitats it needed were lost, leading to the extinction of the species. When habitat change or destruction is an influence for extinction, it might be because that habitat is completely removed, or maybe poisoned or its temperature has changed. A whole host of changes to a habitat can bring about an extinction event.

CLIMATE CHANGE

We hear a lot now about how climate change is leading to many extinctions, but it has long been a leading cause of species disappearing for millions of years.

One example is the Irish elk, or *Megaloceros* (mega loss-serr-oss), a large deer species once found all across Asia and Europe (including Ireland, as you might expect). The population started to fall during the last ice age and the elks finally died out around 7,500 years ago. With so many changes to the climate, their habitat altered. With less habitat and poorer quality food, numbers dropped because there wasn't enough to eat. They also dropped over time because less food and less habitat meant the species itself became less healthy, and had fewer and weaker young. Climate change, and a final nudge from human hunting, destroyed the Irish elk.

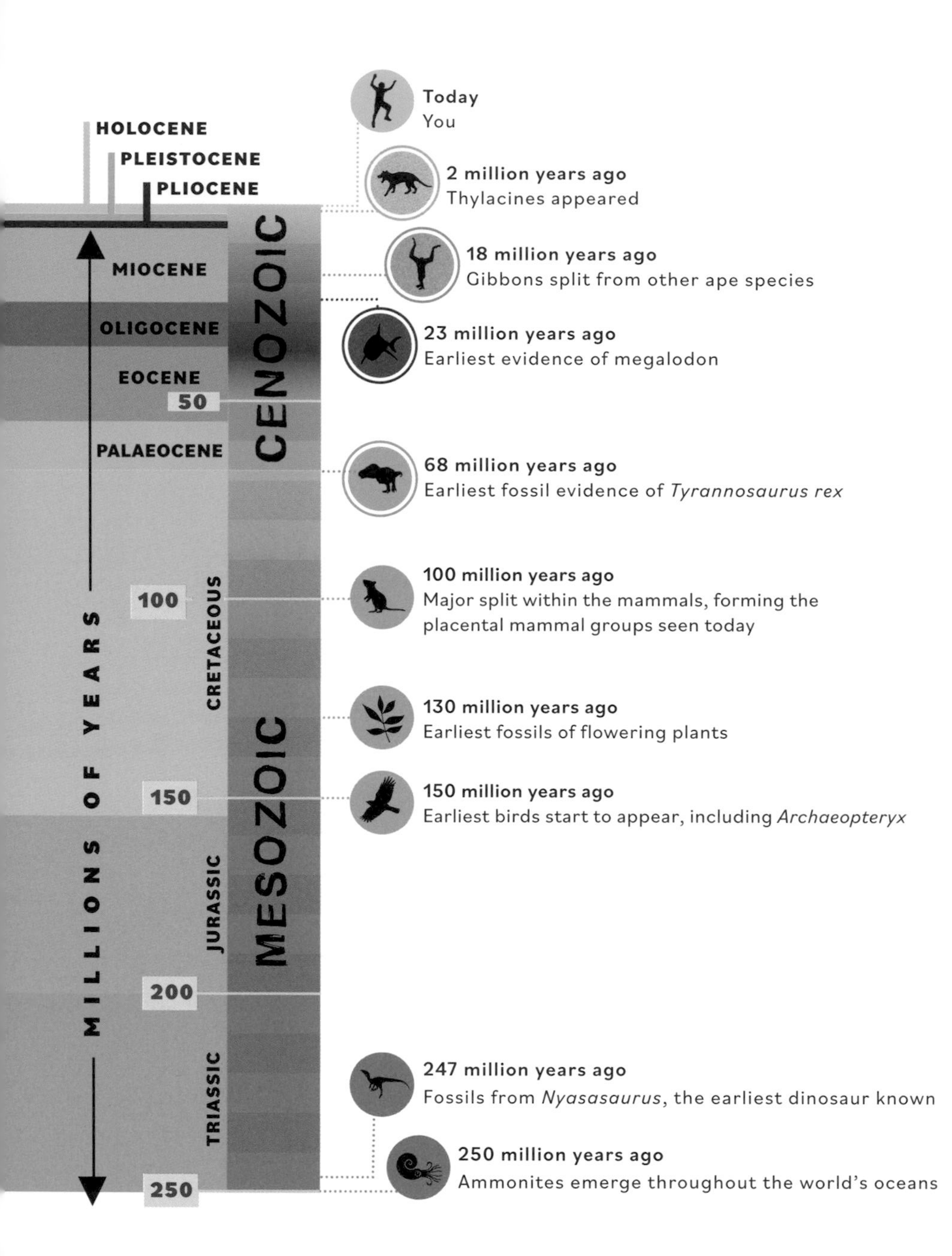
HOLOCENE
PLEISTOCENE
PLIOCENE
MIOCENE
OLIGOCENE
EOCENE
50
PALAEOCENE
CENOZOIC
100
CRETACEOUS
150
MESOZOIC
JURASSIC
200
TRIASSIC
250
MILLIONS OF YEARS
Today
You
2 million years ago
Thylacines appeared
18 million years ago
Gibbons split from other ape species
23 million years ago
Earliest evidence of megalodon
68 million years ago
Earliest fossil evidence of Tyrannosaurus rex
100 million years ago
Major split within the mammals, forming the placental mammal groups seen today
130 million years ago
Earliest fossils of flowering plants
150 million years ago
Earliest birds start to appear, including Archaeopteryx
247 million years ago
Fossils from Nyasasaurus, the earliest dinosaur known
250 million years ago
Ammonites emerge throughout the world's oceans

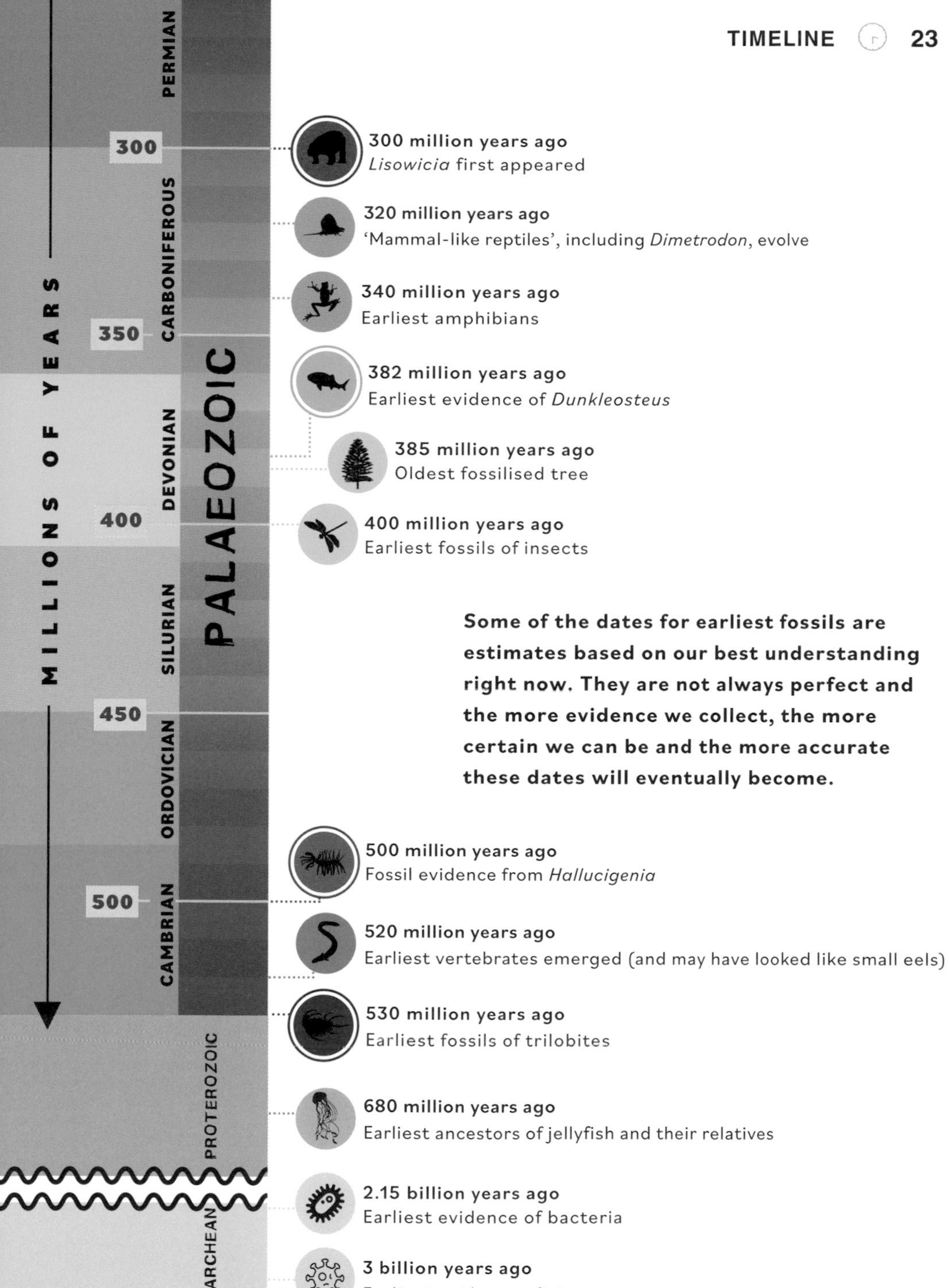

Some of the dates for earliest fossils are estimates based on our best understanding right now. They are not always perfect and the more evidence we collect, the more certain we can be and the more accurate these dates will eventually become.

MASS EXTINCTIONS

RIGHT NOW, somewhere in the world, something, for some reason, will be going extinct, hopefully due to natural causes. In the same way that the evolution and appearance of a species is completely natural, so too is the constant loss of species. Species come and go in a cycle, a bit like tides moving back and forth or the changing of the seasons.

Extinction is unavoidable and goes on at a fairly predictable rate wherever life exists. We call this background extinction: constant, low-level extinction which doesn't cause major problems on a wider scale, other than for the species going extinct, that is. These 'every day extinctions' go mostly unnoticed by the majority of us.

This all changes when we talk about a mass extinction. For the purposes of my books, we are going to treat a mass extinction as the worldwide loss of around 75 per cent (or more) of species, over a short space of 'geological' time.

If you're wondering how short 'a short space of geological time' is, then let's say it has to be under three million years. This might sound a very long time, but remember Earth is around four and a half *billion* years old. By making our timeframe three million years we catch the sudden disastrous mass extinctions, such as the dinosaur-killing asteroid End Cretaceous event, as well as some of the mass extinctions which played out over hundreds of thousands or even millions of years ago.

Mass extinctions, as you might expect, involve loss of life on a huge scale, either across a large number of species or groups, or across a significant part of the planet, or both. In a mass extinction event, the rate of species being lost is greater than the rate by which species are evolving. Imagine you're slowly filling a bucket with water, but there's a big hole in its side; over time, the bucket will still become empty.

Over the last 500 million years or so, the Earth has experienced multiple mass extinctions, ranging from five to as many as 20, depending on what definitions (and there are a number of different ones) scientists use.

In the worst of these mass extinction events, over 90 per cent of life on Earth has been wiped out, and in terms of life recovering to a level from before the event, it may take at least 10 million years for biodiversity levels to return to what they were.

Some mass extinctions, like the one caused by the asteroid 66 million years ago at the end of the Cretaceous period, are pretty quick, while others spread across hundreds of thousands of years to take full effect.

When we talk about mass extinctions, most scientists agree there are five classic mass extinctions, with the earliest occurring around 450 million years ago and the most recent 66 million years ago. In addition to these famous five mass extinctions, another was identified recently, which struck around 2.5 million years ago.

Now, many scientists say we are entering (or even in) the sixth mass extinction event, but this is something which needs to be looked at closely for two reasons. First, I've mentioned the recently identified mass extinction which occurred just over two million years ago, which would make that the sixth mass extinction, so the current global extinction event would be the seventh, in fact.

Second, as we'll see later in the series, it's really hard to say exactly when most mass extinctions start, so, as bad as it is right now, we may not even be in one yet.

Throughout the series, we're going to look at the five classic mass extinctions, the newly discovered mass extinction and the current extinction event, which is being triggered by us. Finally, we'll look at how scientists and conservationists are tackling the threat of extinction now and explore what can be done.

THE LATE DEVONIAN MASS EXTINCTION

AFTER THE FIRST mass extinction which affected animals, at the end of the Ordovician (or-doe vish-EE-an) period, life started to recover. Many new species and groups of species evolved, first in the Silurian (SIY lurr-EE-an) period and then the Devonian (dev own-EE-an) period, which followed. The Silurian and Devonian were two periods in the middle of the large stretch of time called the Palaeozoic (PAY-LEE-O zo-ik) era, which lasted from

541 million years ago to 252.2 million years ago. This came before the more familiar Mesozoic (mez-O zo-ik) era with its three well-known periods: the Triassic (TRI-ass ik), Jurassic (jurr-ass ik) and Cretaceous (cret-AY shuss).

Although some groups survived the Ordovician mass extinction, others evolved, changed and diversified into different shapes and sizes. They developed new behaviours, living in new niches entirely or within ecological gaps left by the previous mass extinction. For example, if all the animals which lived near the surface disappeared, but that part of the environment remained a good place to live, then another group will evolve to fill that 'gap'. A group which did just this across marine and other aquatic habitats was the fish, and for that reason, the Devonian period is often called 'The Age of the Fishes'.

Like the one before it, this mass extinction had a huge and devastating impact on marine habitats, but this time, far more groups and species of fish were impacted. Not only did this mass extinction stand out because it almost completely eradicated the oceans' fishes but it was also unlike any other mass extinction in that it was *not a single event*. There wasn't an asteroid with an immediate tsunami, and there wasn't a deep space explosion with killer radiation rays. This mass extinction took a long time. It took years. In fact, the Late Devonian mass extinction took almost 20 million years from the moment it started to the point when our oceans were nearly entirely emptied.

Usually, when a geological period ends with a mass extinction, its name starts with the word 'end', such as the End Ordovician, the End Triassic and the End Cretaceous. The Late Devonian is different, because it started way before the end of the Devonian period; 20 million years before, in fact. Throughout this mass extinction, there were many spikes of loss, where, for whatever reason, species and groups of species disappeared, but the start and end of the Late Devonian mass extinction each underwent a huge event of loss.

Life on Earth had already started experiencing higher than usual numbers of extinctions when, 374 million years ago, the Kellwasser (kell wass-er) event occurred. Even on its own, this would have been big enough to be classed as a mass extinction without the contribution of the next 20 million years. This 'spike' towards the start of the Late Devonian mass extinction was responsible for wiping out 90 per cent of the largest reefs that have ever existed. Over the next 20 million years a series of losses ended with the Hangenberg (hann-gen burg) event, 359 million years ago. This was the full stop of the Late Devonian mass extinction and in this major spike, most of the large marine species which had done so well to survive were killed off.

CAUSES

The Late Devonian mass extinction is, possibly, the longest mass extinction recorded, spanning an almost unbelievable 20 million years. Although not every palaeontologist agrees that the Late Devonian mass extinction is a single event and think it should instead be seen as several mass extinctions lumped together, most see it as a very slow event, with multiple episodes and spikes of extinction. Not only does this mean it would have been devastating but, for scientists hoping to study it now, it is also an exciting challenge to untangle what happened when, which events triggered extinctions and even when particular species and groups were lost.

Imagine getting home from school and your mum or dad asks you how your day was. Your conversation might go a little bit like this:

Mum/Dad: 'How was your day?'
You: 'It was awful.'
Mum/Dad: 'Oh, that's a shame, why was it so bad?'
You: 'Well, it was raining and when I walked to the bus stop, I stepped in a puddle. Then the bus was late, so I was late and the teacher was angry. I accidentally left my lunch on the bus and then forgot we had a science test and I hadn't revised. During the test, a bee flew in at the window and stung me on the thumb, and on the way home, I skidded on a banana skin and fell over.'

Mum/Dad: 'So which *one* of these things meant you had a bad day?'

If all that actually happened, no wonder you'd be having a bad day, but it would be very difficult to pinpoint which one thing made the day 'bad'. It would more than likely be a combination of some or all of them. This is similar to what happened with the Late Devonian mass extinction. With so many areas of uncertainty surrounding mass extinctions, scientists need clues to piece together what actually happened.

Looking at the physical evidence and climate at the time is a good place to start. If you opened a window now and sampled the air outside, you would discover that around 21 per cent of the air we breathe is made up of oxygen. Throughout the Devonian period though, the level of oxygen was approximately 13 per cent, which dropped to 10 per cent at the end of the period. Less oxygen meant more of other gases. Many of these greenhouse gases in high concentration produced a warmer atmosphere. Overall, the Earth would have been warmer throughout the Devonian and the temperature would have continued to increase up until the end of the period, some 358.9 million years ago.

Because the planet would have been warmer overall, there would have been less of a difference between conditions along the equator and those at the poles, than we see today between tropical habitats and Arctic and Antarctic environments. Instead, tropical equatorial conditions filled a much wider belt, reaching higher and lower latitudes than now.

Knowing what the atmosphere was made up from definitely helps us piece together palaeoenvironments. While disagreement surrounding the Late Devonian mass extinction remains, scientists are in agreement that a combination of rising sea levels, global warming and a reduction in the amount of oxygen in the atmosphere (anoxia), all played a part at the end of the Age of the Fishes. But what caused all these changes, why did this extinction take millions of years and how did it kill nearly all the fish on the planet?

I want you to do a quick experiment: think of a group of organisms which live on land and have been immensely successful. You might think of the dinosaurs, with massive predators such as *Giganotosaurus* and towering giants like the *Patagotitan*. Or maybe the mammals: from those aerial acrobats the horseshoe bats, to our very own species.

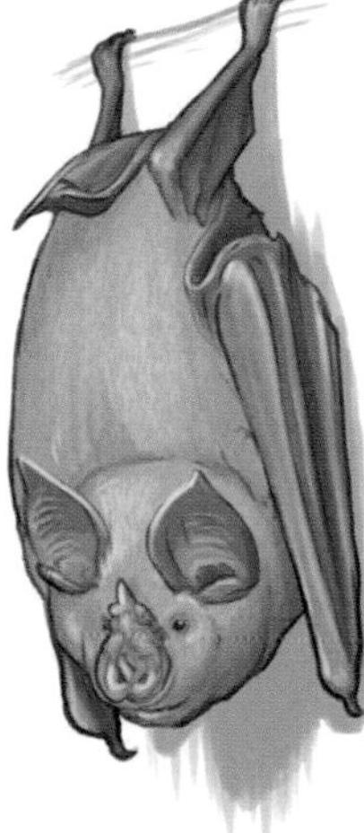

What about plants, though? Were they on your list of top three successful groups of organisms? I thought not. It's all too easy to overlook plants and take them for granted, but they are essential for life if you live on land.

For hundreds of millions of years, land was a dry and barren place, inhospitable and without life. During the Ordovician period, plants first made it on land and even then, it would be hard to describe them as impressive. You might have recognised early examples of mosses and liverworts, which still grow between damp plant pots in forgotten parts of gardens. But once plants began to colonise land, they thrived, evolved and quickly became a very diverse group.

Different species of plants competed for space and resources, but they remained small for millions of years. There would have been no large ferns, bamboo, grasses or bushes and there definitely wouldn't have been any trees. Across almost all of the planet, you would not have been able to find a single plant that grew higher than your knees!

This all changed in the Devonian period. The first tall plants weren't quite trees, but did look like palm trees, even though they didn't have roots as we might know them. Early trees appeared and started pushing their roots into the ground, anchoring them securely and drawing water and nutrients from the soil.

Before long, the first forests formed, teeming with the first insects and other early terrestrial invertebrates. Activity on land exploded and life on Earth would never be the same again. It would go from strength to strength, but there would be a terrible cost for this early terrestrial exploration, because, while we have a lot to be grateful to trees for, they nearly killed all life on Earth during the Late Devonian, around 375 million years ago.

To explain how the evolution of trees and plants is linked to the extinction of nearly everything in these ancient oceans, I'm going to use a slightly strange example from my own garden. About a year ago, I found a beautiful old white ceramic sink on my street. It was very heavy, but I managed to get it home and placed it outside my kitchen door. I glued a plug in place, added a layer of stones in the bottom and filled it with water.

Before long, it had water 'fleas' and aquatic snails, some pond plants such as horsetails and the clearest water I've ever seen in a pond. Understandably, I was very proud of it. I bought a nice plant for my tiny pond at a local garden centre. It was in a pot full of muddy soil to help the little yellow-flowered plant grow. I sat back and waited eagerly for it to bloom.

Instead, about a week later, the pond was thick with bright green algae. Every day, I'd grab handfuls of the stuff. It was everywhere. I wasn't able to clean the pond for a few days and when I returned, there was so much weed, it had choked the pond. Some of the plants I did want in the pond weren't looking too healthy and sadly, most of the invertebrates were dead. The empty snail shells were covered in algae.

I turned detective to see what had caused this. The culprit was that pot with the yellow-flowering plant. When I placed it in the pond, there must have been too many nutrients in the soil. They were released into the water and instantly drawn up by the plants that were able to act the fastest – the algae. But the algae used up the valuable oxygen in the water and died too, completing my small-scale extinction event.

This process, where excess nutrients cause an algal bloom which then dies and causes a major drop in the level of oxygen, is called eutrophication (YOO-tro fik-KAY shun) and can affect streams, rivers and lakes. It can also have a devastating impact on marine habitats.

When algal blooms happen in a coastal environment, maybe because fertilisers on farmland have washed into rivers and down to the sea, they can kill life for hundreds or even thousands of kilometres. Imagine what a worldwide series of giant algal blooms would do to the word's marine ecosystems.

A global algal bloom appears to have occurred towards the end of the Devonian period, when the first trees with proper roots evolved. Possibly, *Archaeopteris* (ark-EE op-terr-iss) was the first true tree (as we understand trees) to exist, and might have grown taller than a house. It would have had roots deep in the ground, where they broke up rock and created soil. This would have been the first soil ever to have existed and so packed with nutrients. So many nutrients, that they appear to have washed into the shallow marine habitats all around the supercontinents. This caused a *huge* algal bloom, draining marine habitats of oxygen around the world.

And the evolution of trees did something else, which added to the catastrophic devastation. They made the world go cold. Plants take in carbon dioxide from the atmosphere, so it makes sense that more plants means less carbon dioxide in the atmosphere. Because carbon dioxide acts as a greenhouse gas, trapping warm air that's been heated by the sun, if there's less of it, then heat can't be trapped as easily and before long, the world is getting a little chilly.

The problem we have now with climate change is that higher and higher levels of carbon dioxide, along with other gases, are making the planet warmer and warmer. But the opposite is also true. Some scientists predict that as much as 90 per cent of the carbon dioxide in the Devonian period atmosphere disappeared.

Trees and other modern plants might look simple, but they are complex organisms, each a mixture of adaptations beautifully combined to help them thrive and survive. But each adaptation took time to evolve. They did not happen at once. Even things we might take for granted, like seeds and roots, evolved at different points in time. These steps in botanical evolution may have been linked to another big release of nutrients into the ground and therefore to all the smaller spikes of extinctions for the duration of the Late Devonian mass extinction.

Algal blooms spread across the planet and choked the life out of marine ecosystems. Here, a huge *Dunkleosteus* has washed up in the shallows, a victim of these toxic plants.

There are scientists who disagree with this global cooling theory and instead, think we saw some global warming and a rise in sea levels. Why is there disagreement about whether the world was cooler and the sea levels dropped, or the world was warmer and the sea levels rose? It's partly because there are still gaps in our understanding – we don't have enough fossils to know exactly what happened and of the fossils we do have, many are incomplete or just small fragments.

Imagine doing a million-piece jigsaw with just a few hundred pieces. To make it worse, some of the pieces are ripped or faded, and others look as though they might be from a completely different puzzle. That's sort of what's going on when we try to piece together a complex event like a 20-million-year extinction event which occurred over 360 million years ago.

It's also because looking at evidence from geology, such as estimating the exact age of rocks which are over 360 million years old, is really difficult. If you're off by even a few thousand years (which is a blink of an eye in terms of evolution and even less when we think about geological processes), then all your results, assumptions and ideas might be completely wrong. Some scientists believe it wasn't plants that were responsible but instead, a series of volcanic eruptions, which caused sea levels to rise and the temperature to increase. It's a great theory and it might be more relevant for a later mass extinction, but there's no real evidence that this was the cause behind the Late Devonian mass extinction.

Until scientists have more evidence, we cannot be certain, especially when trying to understand a specific part of Earth's history over a quarter of a billion years ago. At the moment, although we don't exactly know what caused the first major spike that marked the start of the Late Devonian mass extinction, it does seem that we can say with some certainty that trees were at least responsible for the second major wave of losses at the end of the event.

I believe the evidence of huge glaciers covering almost the entire planet makes it look as though trees were responsible for high levels of nutrients being dumped into the seas and also for a massive drop in the levels of carbon dioxide. First, the nutrients caused too much algae, which when it died suffocated the oceans of oxygen. When those same trees used up a large proportion of the carbon dioxide in the air, the following ice age helped finish off millions of Devonian marine species.

This is the only mass extinction we know of (so far) where plants were responsible for the death and destruction of species and ecosystems across the planet. It's hard to look at your garden or playing field the same way again when you understand the extent of the devastation caused, nearly wiping out animal life, just as it was ready to leave the water.

Hallipterus excelsior

EFFECTS

85

The Late Devonian mass extinction during 'The Age of the Fishes' was different to the extinction event we saw at the end of the Ordovician period in many ways. A key difference was that previously fish were a small part of the marine ecosystem, while the Devonian period saw a dazzling assortment of fish, in different shapes and sizes, covering every part of the food chain, from bottom-feeding detritivores, to large predatory sharks.

In the Devonian, the seas were full of fish, from huge, armoured predators such as *Dunkleosteus* and their smaller relatives *Bothriolepis*, to shoals of large, sleek *Hyneria*.

On the land, as new habitats were forming, strange 8m-tall fungi *Prototaxites* towers dominated some landscapes.

The Devonian was also different in that terrestrial habitats had become established and were continuing to develop. A range of plants colonised the land, followed by insects, the first animals to exploit land-based ecosystems. The land cover across the Earth had continued to change during the Early Devonian period, due to the influence of tectonic activity, through the slow but immensely powerful movement and crashing together of the huge plates deep within our planet's crust. The supercontinent Gondwana began to break up and new land masses started to form a new giant continent called Eumerica (YOO mer-rik-aar) from smaller pieces of land.

The results created some spectacular mountain ranges which can still be seen today, including the Appalachian (appa LAY-SHE-an) Mountains (in Canada and North America) and the Caledonian (kal-EE doh-NEE-an) mountain range (which stretches from North America and Greenland, to Scotland and across Norway). Now, close to 70 per cent of the surface of the Earth is covered by oceans, but back in the Late Devonian, this was as high as 85 per cent. It really was a watery world.

This is how the Earth looked in the Late Devonian period.

Things were going well for life on the Earth during the Devonian period. But that all changed, starting approximately 374 million years ago when the Earth witnessed its second mass extinction. Then, it is estimated, between 80 and 90 per cent of marine species were lost, with around 20 per cent of marine families going extinct.

This is important, because if a family of organisms with 10 species, for example, loses eight of them in a mass extinction, there will still be two species left, but if the whole family disappears, then there will be no representative species from this group and the whole evolutionary line stops. When 20 per cent of all marine families were lost in the Late Devonian mass extinction, this meant that one in five groups of marine organisms were lost forever.

Many species and groups of brachiopods, sponges, trilobites and cephalopods were lost during the Late Devonian mass extinction. Many of the strange, marine, scorpion-like eurypterids (YOO-rip ter-idz) were also lost.

It was the Late Devonian mass extinction, however, that kickstarted the process which would go on to produce much of the natural gas we use today, some 360 million years or so later. The hundreds of millions of marine plants and animals which died around the world formed a sludgy layer of death on seabeds, which, as they continued to decompose, released gas. This became trapped, until it was extracted by humans millions of years later and used to help power our modern world.

Now, we rely on energy to power our complex modern societies and while some of it comes from renewable sources, such as wind farming and forms of solar energy, much of it still comes from fossil fuels, such as coal, oil and natural gases. These fossil fuels are not limitless and they will run out.

Although there were two major peaks of loss within this mass extinction event, there were possibly 10 or more separate episodes of loss within the 20-million-year period, making the Late Devonian mass extinction the only extinction event to take place over such a prolonged time and to have so many different episodes or parts to it. It's amazing that anything at all made it through.

ASK THE EXPERT

Dr Tom Fletcher is an Honorary Fellow at the University of Leicester and also makes wildlife and science documentaries. He is a palaeontologist who has studied ancient sharks by looking at the way their skin helped them to swim effortlessly and to survive for hundreds of millions of years.

Why is biodiversity important?

If you visit a zoo, safari park or nature reserve, you'll see a whole host of different animals, but they are just the icing on a very large cake. Maybe, over 99.999 per cent of the species out there in the world are yet to be discovered and no one knows how many millions, billions, or even trillions of species actually exist.

So why is it so difficult to count them? Some species are incredibly rare, some so similar that we can't tell them apart, and some so small that it is difficult to find them in the first place. For example, there are around 10,000 different species of bacteria in a gram of soil, and it's a huge job working out who's who.

We know from the fossil record that the number of different species - which we call biodiversity - has risen and fallen over time. It rises when species gradually evolve to survive in their own separate ways, and over time we get lots of new species interacting with each other in ecosystems like rainforests or coral reefs. Each ecosystem is like a stage play with lots of actors performing their parts, each with their own skills and specialisations. The fossil record tells us that life isn't always easy and sometimes the play goes wrong.

One example of this is when a mass extinction wipes out most of the cast. When species in the play disappear, it's up to the survivors to perform the old parts that make the system work. If there aren't many actors around, there's less chance of the roles being filled. Doing a school play with 20 actors is hard but doing that same play with five actors taking multiple parts is much, much harder. Instead, other actors who don't have the skills or specialisations have to evolve slowly to fill the gaps in the ecosystem, like learning a completely new script.

The meteorite that killed most of the dinosaurs was devastating at the time, but there were lots of small mammals and birds ready to take the place of the dinosaurs, and ecosystems recovered well. So increased biodiversity means ecosystems can bounce back faster and the play can go on, even if there are slightly different actors playing the roles each time.

We are living through one of the worst extinctions the world has ever seen, and we are only just beginning to understand our power to disturb the natural order. Some of the problems are obvious, like habitat destruction, climate change and pollution. But there are lots of other ways biodiversity can suffer. Humans have been moving species that would never normally meet each other across the globe for centuries. The aggressive species that can adapt and reproduce quickly outcompete those that are stuck in their ways and living in the slow lane. As we mix up the rainbow colours of species on Earth, we end up with nothing but brown, one colour where there used to be many. With that loss of biodiversity and those lost actors, we lose the safety net of all the ecosystems on our planet, which is why it is vital we protect it.

DUNKLEOSTEUS

FOR ME, the ocean and the habitats which surround it have always offered a sense of comfort and belonging. I've never been scared of the sea or anything in it, and have been lucky enough to see majestic tiger sharks and huge humpback whales up close. But had I been diving in those same seas some 360 million years ago, I think I would have been terrified.

Millions of years before whales evolved or before there were any large sharks, the world's first super-predator swam there. When we look at a food chain, there are often a couple of layers of predators, sometimes with one type of hunter going after another, but when there are no more levels above a certain predator, it can be said to be at the top of the food chain. It's what we call an apex predator, the ultimate predator in that ecosystem. And the first apex predator wasn't just the ultimate predator in its environment but would have been the ultimate killer *anywhere* on the planet. Back in the Devonian, the deadliest predator the world had ever known was *Dunkleosteus*.

DISCOVERY

If I asked you to conjure the deadliest marine predators, which would appear in your mind? Go on, try it. A great white shark? Obviously. The killer whale? Oh, nice! A pliosaur? Great – you're going old-school now! The oceans around the world have been home to some of the most terrifying and mighty predators that nature has to offer, from the speedy ichthyosaurs and ravenous bull sharks to giant squid-munching sperm whales.

It's as if marine habitats around the world are the perfect playground for evolutionary experiments and, if evolution did have an imagination, oceans would be the place where it was allowed to go a bit wild.

But let's go back to before toothed whales appeared and earlier than the first predatory prehistoric marine reptiles – further into prehistory than even the large sharks we see today. Back to a time when mammals were a far-off daydream and even the ancient sharks were still relatively small and not the impressive predators they would later become. There was, however, a giant predator dominating the oceans. It was the biggest predator that, up until that point, had ever existed. It was the first super-predator, the first apex predator. It was *Dunkleosteus*.

The infamous, ancient and armoured *Dunkleosteus* existed at a time when animals were first evolving to move on to the land. To be fair, if I was an ancient fish with fins that could be used as legs, I'd have given the land a go too, just so that I never had to meet *Dunkleosteus* underwater. There was nothing else like this marine monster then and there hasn't been since. We have some great fossils, but there is still so much about this iconic predator we don't know. Why did it need to be so big? What did its body look like? Was it *really* a cannibal?

The giant predatory *Dunkleosteus* ate absolutely anything it could find. Many fossils from this species show damage around the head, which could only have come from a larger *Dunkleosteus*, meaning these super-predators were also cannibals.

Very often in palaeontology, a new species is discovered by someone who is not an expert, and it is not found as a complete skeleton. This is exactly what happened with *Dunkleosteus*. The first fossils were discovered in 1867 by Jay Terrell and his son. Mr Terrell owned a hotel but he was also an amateur palaeontologist. There are thousands of amateur palaeontologists around the world collecting fossils, sometimes finding new species. It's so important for there to be a strong relationship between fossil hunters, university researchers and museums, because when we work together, we all benefit from the amazing discoveries in a scientific and accurate way.

After finding the fossils around the shores of Lake Erie in Ohio, in the northeastern part of the USA, Mr Terrell and his son realised the bones came from a pretty formidable-looking fish, so they called it the *Terrible Fish*. The fossils were fragments of a huge bony head from a huge prehistoric fish, belonging to a group of extinct armoured fish called the placoderms (plak-OH dermz). The name means 'plated skin'.

Over the next 50 years or so, not many new fossils of *Dunkleosteus* were found. But, in the 1920s, when mechanical steam diggers excavated the area where the original discovery was made in order to improve water drainage and flood prevention in the region, many more specimens were found. In 1928, two museum curators from the recently formed Cleveland Museum of Natural History, found the fossil of a Terrible Fish that was larger and more complete than any discovered before. They spent the next eight years delicately cleaning away rock attached to the fragile fossil bone of the skull and piecing it back together.

It was only in 1956, almost a hundred years after the first discovery, that the Terrible Fish was given its official, scientific name. The name *Dunkleosteus* (Dun-kll oss-tee-us) literally means 'Dunkle bone'. It was named after Dr David Dunkle, the palaeontologist who was the first museum curator to work with the specimens in detail. The word 'osteus', from the Greek for 'bone', refers to the giant bone plates that make up the head and jaws.

Several species have now been discovered and scientifically described, but the first, and largest, is called *Dunkleosteus terrelli*, in honour of Mr Jay Terrell.

ANATOMY

I'm going to try to read your mind. Let's see how good I am. If I asked you to physically describe *Dunkleosteus*, and say three things about it, I can almost guarantee one will be wrong. I predict the three things you'd mention are that it was a huge fish, that it had an armoured head and very big, sharp teeth. Am I right?

It was a bit of a trick, really, because *Dunkleosteus* is famous for these three things, but its most famous feature are not teeth! It didn't have teeth. Or fangs, if you're trying to outsmart me.

Teeth are specific structures in the mouths of lots of different animals. They're made from different materials, including enamel and dentine, but not from bone. Some teeth, including those of many fish and reptiles, are attached directly to the bone of the jaw, but a tooth is not made from bone.

Dunkleosteus, despite having what looked like two massive fangs on each jaw and what looked like four sets of sharp, shearing cheek teeth, was completely tooth-free. Instead, it used the bone of the jaw itself to hunt and kill its food. These plates of bone rubbed against each other and would have continuously sharpened themselves throughout the animal's life.

Although we will get to describing *Dunkleosteus* in detail, we're going to start with trying to answer one of the most fascinating questions about this prehistoric predator – just how powerful was it? It is clear very quickly that *Dunkleosteus* was an immensely strong animal. You can tell that just by looking at it but, in science, we like to be a little more specific. How strong was the bite force of this fear-inducing fish?

Figuring out the power an animal uses to bite can be surprisingly tricky, for a few reasons. Would you want to put your hand anywhere near the mouth of a 3m-long crocodile? No, me neither. What about attaching electrodes to a great white shark? Didn't think so. Even if you do manage to attach the equipment, how do you know the animal is actually biting properly? Some of the equipment used to measure bite force looks like a rubber ring or bar, which might not make the animal use its whole potential. And even if you can attach the scientific equipment and make the animal bite it properly, then how are you supposed to measure this in an animal which has gone extinct and lived hundreds of millions of years ago? Like I said, it's tricky.

We measure force in a unit called newtons (or N) and, as you might expect, the higher the number, the greater the bite force. Let's start with us. An adult human bite force is around 890N. The bone-crushing hyena has a much more impressive bite force of about 2,000N. And research shows that a great white shark may be able to bite as much as 18,000N and a *Tyrannosaurus rex* might have had a phenomenal bite force of 50,000N. When palaeontologists teamed up with

engineers to see what bite force *Dunkleosteus* was able to produce, they estimated it had a powerful bite, around 7,400N, so not quite as much as some people might expect.

But before you start to feel disappointed, *Dunkleosteus* did have another trick up its sleeve, which made this already impressive, but not record-breaking, bite into something that was truly deadly. Usually, an animal has either a large bite force, or the ability to bite quickly. We rarely see both. This is where *Dunkleosteus* was an exception. Its jaws could snap shut in an incredible 20 milliseconds. One millisecond is a thousandth of a second. If you're wondering how fast that is, the quickest reaction time you have is around 250 milliseconds.

Research has shown that, incredibly, *Dunkleosteus* may have been able to snap its jaws five times faster than you can blink. Being able to close its jaws that fast, coupled with a bite force of 7,400N, was a combination so deadly that *Dunkleosteus* would have been able to bite through skin, muscle and bone. Bizarrely, it also meant this aquatic predator might have used suction to feed.

Dunkleosteus's skull was like a mechanical trap – similar to the jagged-toothed traps we often see in cartoons. But rather than having one joint where movement takes place, the head of *Dunkleosteus* possessed four different sites where movement occurred. You have one joint in your skull – it's at the point where your jaw meets the rest of the skull. By adding another three joints, *Dunkleosteus* was able to throw its entire face forwards extremely rapidly and the process of opening and closing the jaws took about 60 milliseconds. This superfast movement would have generated a pressure difference between what was inside the mouth and what was outside, meaning when the mouth was opened, it would have created suction, drawing prey closer to, or even inside, the deadly jaws.

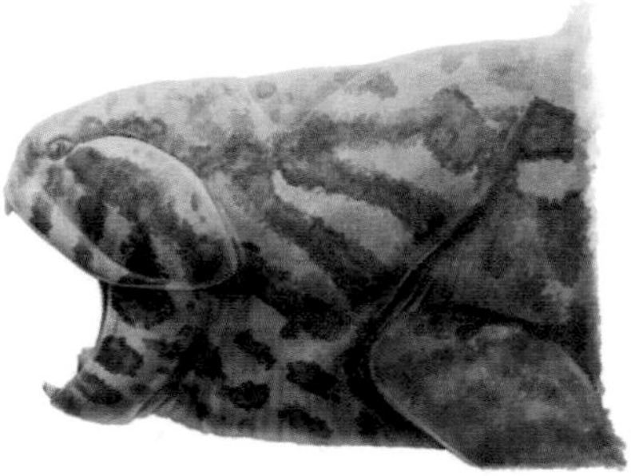

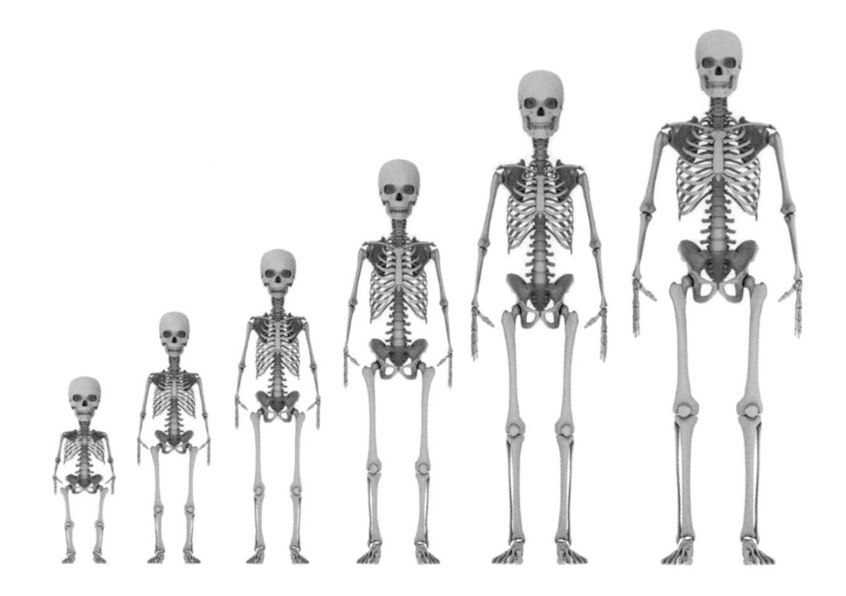

Now, let's consider size. You may not have noticed this or may never have thought about it, but when you're little, you're not just a smaller version of an adult. If you took a photo of a toddler and used a computer to scale the image up to the size of an adult, it would look really strange. In the first image above, you can see the human skeleton at different ages through our life, from about 18 months old through to adulthood. You'll see that as we age, the skull accounts for a smaller amount of the whole body length.

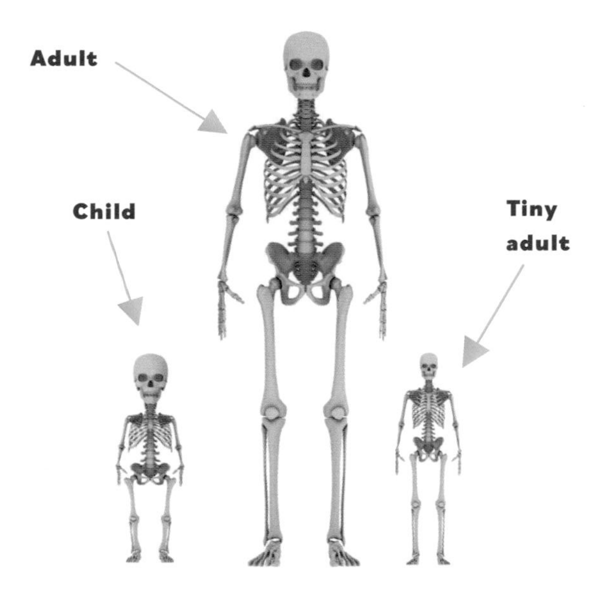

The second image shows what happens when you shrink an adult human skeleton to the size of an 18-month-old child. It looks weird. As organisms age, for many, it's a case of not just getting bigger overall, but a change in the proportions of the body. The same can be said for *Dunkleosteus*. Scientists discovered from fossils that as this animal grew, the proportions of the skull changed, not just the overall size.

It is hard to predict accurate estimates of body length and the weight of an animal if you only find parts of the fossil. Although palaeontologists have found some impressive *Dunkleosteus* fossils, most are from the head. This means there will always be some uncertainty over statements made about other parts of the body, but the more fossils we find, the more certain we shall become.

So far, scientists predict that an average adult *Dunkleosteus* would have been around 6m long, which is about the same as a saltwater crocodile, and would have weighed around a tonne, similar to a black rhino. However, the very largest fossil may have belonged to an individual 879cm long, which is nearly 9m (about the same as two family cars back to back) in length. Even if we look at some of the most impressive ocean predators alive today, we can

see *Dunkleosteus* would have made its mark, being longer than a great white shark, which can reach 6m in length, or even a killer whale, which can be up to 8m long. Despite being longer, it appears *Dunkleosteus* did not weigh as much as some of our present-day predators. A big great white shark can weigh around 2 tonnes and a killer whale can be as much as 6 tonnes.

What did *Dunkleosteus* look like?

Dunkleosteus is one of the most well-known and recognised prehistoric fish from around 360 million years ago, but what do we know about its appearance? We know lots about its head. The self-sharpening sheaths of bone in its mouth and the heavily armoured skull give it a distinctive appearance and would have helped make *Dunkleosteus* one of the first apex predators anywhere on the planet. But we have very few fossil remains from other parts of its body, which has led to disagreement between scientists over the years. Was it a very long fish, like an armour-headed eel? Did it have the flat body of a ray or the streamlined shape of a tuna?

A shoal of *Stethacanthus* is joined by a single *Dunkleosteus* in open water. Devonian sharks and other fish looked very different to sea life we encounter in our oceans today.

Around 95 per cent of the *Dunkleosteus* fossils found so far have less than a quarter of their skeleton preserved. The only things scientists could rely on when *Dunkleosteus* was discovered were the fossils from much smaller, related armoured fish. Some of the best preserved of these were from species which did have an eel-like body but were usually only around 25cm long.

It didn't feel right for the one-tonne *Dunkleosteus* to look like a bigger version of its much smaller freshwater cousins, but we only found the answer more recently. A well-preserved fossil was discovered, with not only the pectoral fin intact, but also the strips of protein filaments which would have sat at the base of the fin. This fossil allowed palaeontologists to understand that the group of armoured fish to which *Dunkleosteus* belonged (the placoderms) swam in lots of different ways and that their anatomy would have been closely tied to their individual way of swimming.

It was in 2017 that researchers were able to confidently predict that *Dunkleosteus* had a more streamlined body, similar to a classic shark shape, and that it would have had a tail with a short lobe at the bottom and a much larger one at the top, a bit like a blue or oceanic whitetip shark. In the largest *Dunkleosteus* individuals, the upper lobe of the tail may have been more than 2m long.

CLASSIFICATION

As with any species, although it's cool to learn all there is about that animal, it is a whole lot cooler (and much more scientific) to learn about its relationships with other species. Was it the only member of a particular group, making it distinct from an evolutionary point of view, or was it just another species among a bigger group of closely related and similar species? How a species evolved and what its family tree looks like can be hugely informative and reveals a huge part of the story for that particular organism. If the same is true for *Dunkleosteus*, it's important to know a little more about what it was related to.

The huge, predatory *Dunkleosteus* belonged to a group of fish called the placoderms. These prehistoric, armoured fish were around for well over 50 million years

Lunaspis

and in that time, the group evolved and diversified in terms of shape, size and their ecological niches. Many were predators, such as the small *Lunaspis* with its whip-like tail, while others were herbivores, including the 1.5m-long algae-eating *Holonema*. Some placoderms,

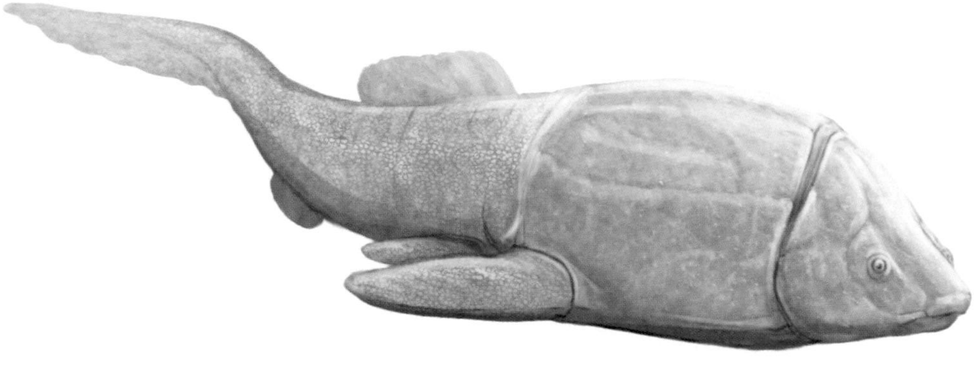

Holonema

Rhenanida

like the 1.5m-long, fast-swimming, predatory *Rolfosteus*, lived in the open water, while the ray-like *Rhenanida* lived on the seabed. There were large filter-feeding *Titanichthys* placoderms which ate plankton, possibly behaving and feeding in a similar way to whale sharks today. And dominating them all was the giant *Dunkleosteus*.

Despite coming in a range of shapes, sizes and behaviours, placoderms were similar in that they all had thick, protective plating covering their heads and the upper part of their bodies. They were, as far as we know, the first group of animals to give birth to live young, rather than depend on egg-laying, which was a very important turning point in the evolutionary history of animals.

Although they are no longer with us, the placoderms are related to all vertebrates alive today that have jaws, but scientists are still not fully certain as to how they're related. Reading this, you might be excited, surprised or even concerned to learn that, if we go back far enough, you might actually be related to the fearsome *Dunkleosteus*!

Although it's easy to think of *Dunkleosteus* as one type of fish, scientists think there may have been eight to 10 different species. Some of these species have been identified from incomplete finds or fragments of fossil bone, so it's practically impossible to be certain whether it really was a different species or not.

The best known *Dunkleosteus* is *Dunkleosteus terrelli*. This was the largest of any *Dunkleosteus* species and was the first to be officially named, back in 1873 – although that name changed to the one we're now familiar with, much later, in the 1950s. It is separated from the others by the rounded shape of its face. Fossils have been found throughout the USA (including in Ohio, Pennsylvania, Tennessee and California) and in Europe.

Other species of *Dunkleosteus* we know about so far include *Dunkleosteus belgicus*, which is known only from a handful of small fossil pieces in Belgium, and seemed to have had a slightly differently shaped scale beneath its eyes, a feature that separates it from its larger cousin. Named in 1885, *Dunkleosteus newberryi* was identified from a lower jawbone discovered in New York (USA). When early palaeontologists found fragments of bone in Missouri (USA) they thought they belonged to *Dunkleosteus terrelli*, but on closer inspection, they realised they were from a separate species. Nearly 60 years after its discovery in New York, *Dunkleosteus magnificus* was recognised as belonging to the group. Before that, scientists believed the fossils belonged to another type of large placoderm, called *Dinichthys*.

Imagine describing a whole species from a single fossil plate on a fish's back, but that's just what happened with *Dunkleosteus denisoni*, when it was described in 1957, from a small fossilised armoured plate. It wasn't even different in shape, just smaller than you might expect for a *Dunkleosteus*. Unlike its larger relatives, *Dunkleosteus raveri* was only around 1m long. When the top of a skull was found in Ohio, scientists were able to see that this species had big eyes. For many fish, having bigger eyes might mean they are nocturnal or live deep in the oceans, where there is little light.

In Canada, remains of *Dunkleosteus amblyodoratus* were identified in 2010. This member of the *Dunkleosteus* group was the same size as its well-known cousin but was different in terms of the shape of the back of the head.

Representing the only possible *Dunkleosteus* remains from Morocco is *Dunkleosteus marsaisi*, but there is some disagreement as to whether it is actually a *Dunkleosteus* or not. Some scientists believe this was a different species, but others think the fossils simply belonged to *Dunkleosteus terrelli*. Others say that these fossils could belong to a different type of placoderm completely. Whatever it was, this fish had a narrower face, extra holes in the skull and was slightly smaller overall.

Although understanding the classification of *Dunkleosteus* is important, it's not easy. We don't really know how placoderms are related to animals alive today, or the relationships between the different placoderms. Even within the *Dunkleosteus* group, it's difficult to understand the different species which did or didn't exist, but as is so often the case with science, the more evidence we have, the more we will know.

ECOLOGY

Every single species has its own ecology, which means the relationship that species has with other species and the interactions it has with its surrounding environment.

Looking at a species on its own doesn't give you the full picture. Imagine if giraffes were extinct and we only understood them from their fossils. If we just looked at the species itself, the long neck would look preposterous and we might have issues understanding why it was so long. But when we look at giraffe ecology, we can reveal the tall trees, which provide leaves for food, and the other herbivores which compete for food and we are able to see why such a long neck might have evolved. This is how understanding an organism's ecology can tell us so much more about the organism itself.

Looking at the ecology of the giraffe seems pretty simple, but when we try to understand a marine ecology from over 360 million years ago, it's rather like trying to explain a magic trick to someone in a language that's not your own – not impossible but not easy, either. And this might sound scary and a little intimidating, but it's actually fascinating and exciting and is what science is all about. Being a scientist is often like solving one detective mystery after another, delving into some of the most intricate mysteries in nature in order to tell some of the most fascinating stories in the universe.

The shallow marine habitats at the time were diverse but overall were dominated by tiny invertebrates, such as filter-feeding bryozoans, which were around half a millimetre in length, and the ancient, double-shelled brachiopods. Crinoids, such as sea lilies and feather stars (which are related to starfish and sea urchins), were common, along with many species of trilobites and early examples of ammonites, which had started appearing during the Early Devonian. There were also a lot of different species of fish throughout the Devonian period. These included the jawless, armoured fish, some of the first sharks and their relatives, and the bony fish, which now includes everything from tuna to sunfish. There were also the placoderms, including *Dunkleosteus*.

During the Devonian, there were lots of coastal habitats and shallow inland seas. The fossil record shows that these tropical inland seas would have lots of minerals and nutrients and other plant material washing into them, all settling on the sea bed. This would have created a stagnant zone low in oxygen, making it difficult, if not impossible, to live there. Because of this, marine life would have instead lived either close to the shoreline or out in open waters.

When

Fossils from *Dunkleosteus* have been found in rocks from the Late Devonian period. Palaeontologists have been able to age these rocks and estimate that *Dunkleosteus* was alive between 382 million years and 359 million years ago.

Where

Although there is a question mark over fossils found in Morocco, which may or may not have belonged to a species of *Dunkleosteus*, the other species have all been found in the shallow seas around the supercontinent Laurasia. Because the continents have now all moved and changed, *Dunkleosteus* fossils are most commonly found in what is now the USA, as well as in Canada and several countries in Europe, including Poland and Belgium.

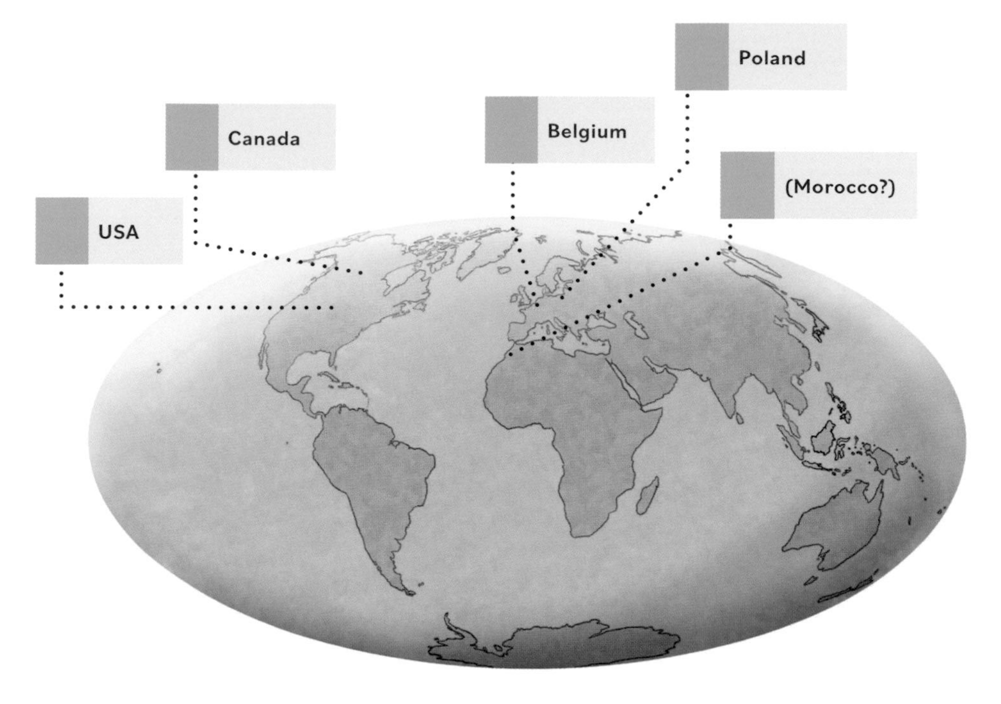

Environment

Earth during the Devonian period would have looked very different to the planet we know so well. It was warmer than today and the sea levels were much higher. We would not have had such a noticeable temperature change as we moved from the equator to the poles, as more of the planet was tropical. The seas and oceans were tropical too and would have been a lot warmer than they are today.

Tectonic plates were shifting and moving together a great deal throughout the Devonian, meaning lots of mountain ranges were created. Overall, the supercontinents were still hot and dry, with near-desert habitats across the land. The coastline was not as dry and many places, such as the zone which now makes up the North American continent, which is where *Dunkleosteus* lived, were dotted with rivers, streams, estuaries and lakes, as well as vast, shallow inland seas. Sea levels were much higher than they are now and, although there were supercontinents, the majority of the planet was covered by one giant ocean, called Panthalassa.

The average level of oxygen within the atmosphere across the Devonian period was 15 per cent, which is three-quarters of what it is today, when it makes up 21 per cent. There was less oxygen but the difference was partly made up by there being more carbon dioxide, as it is believed the levels were over five times higher than they are now. Having higher levels of this greenhouse gas would have caused the planet to be warmer than it is today. On average, the Earth was 20°C, which is five degrees more than the average today.

A hungry *Dunkleosteus* stalks a large *Tegeolepis*. A Devonian shark, *Sphenacanthus*, and a shoal of *Coccosteus*, which are related to *Dunkleosteus*, swim by unaware in the shallows.

Flora and fauna 

The Devonian period was a time of big change, in terms of the species and groups of animals which evolved. It is famous for its fish and we owe our existence to some of these Devonian fishes, but there were many other organisms which weren't fish and lots of species which weren't even marine but were instead venturing onto land.

Many of the organisms alive during the Devonian did not make it through the mass extinction and were lost, but luckily, some didn't go extinct and are still alive today, almost unchanged for over a quarter of a billion years.

If you look at all the fossils of fish from the Late Devonian period, you would quickly notice two things. First, there would be a lot of them and second, the most commonly seen fossil would be from one of the very unusual-looking *Bothriolepis* (both-REE-O lep-iss) fish. Like *Dunkleosteus*, the *Bothriolepis* group were part of the placoderms but their most noticeable features were the long crab-like pincers growing from their sides, which were actually fins. Another fish from the Late Devonian was the famous *coelacanth* (seel-a can-th).

The coelacanth is what's known as a lobe-finned fish, which have pairs of lobe-like fins instead of the flat fins we normally think of on fish. Although most have now died out, this is an incredibly important group, as it is from these that amphibians, reptiles, birds and mammals (which includes us, remember) evolved. If you go back far enough, your great great great great great great great great great great great great – add a few more years of you saying 'great' – great granny was swimming around alongside *Dunkleosteus*.

Although our very own predatory placoderm was a terrifying fish, it wasn't the only impressive Devonian marine carnivore. Sharks were abundant throughout this period but they did not have the classic shark shape. Then, there were some truly fascinating-looking sharks, including the 70cm *Stethacanthus* (steth-a can-thuss), which had a dorsal fin resembling an ironing board or anvil, which may have been used for defence or courtship or for attaching to larger fish, just as remoras do today.

During the Devonian, large filter-feeders like *Titanichthys* and the huge predator *Dunkleosteus* dominated the seas.

Today, healthy oceanic ecosystems attract birds, fish, mammals and invertebrates.

Another ancient shark was the torpedo-like *Cladoselache* (CLAY-doh sell-arch-EE). This group reached nearly 2m in length and were fast, streamlined predators. The ancient sharks of the Devonian period were different to their modern-day descendants in many ways, and *Cladoselache* was no exception. They are one of the few sharks which did not have rough teeth-like scales covering their bodies.

Although many Devonian sharks and other fish were striking in their appearance, it's not a huge leap to imagine their descendants today. But there were some organisms which would have looked like something out of an alien film. For example, the giant eurypterid (YOO-rip ter-id) 'sea scorpions'. With over 250 species, these aquatic arthropods varied in shape and behaviour, and although we are not certain, it appears they would have been active predators. Some eurypterids grew up to 2.5m in length, making them the largest invertebrates ever to have existed.

Whenever I think of the Devonian marine habitats, I always imagine how difficult it would have been to have lived there if I was a small fish. I would have had to survive huge, armoured fish like *Dunkleosteus*, strange, predatory sharks such as *Cladoselache* and other-worldly eurypterids with their deadly claws. I used to imagine that if I was a small fish, I'd certainly have wanted to escape the water and head to land, where there were no large predators and few competitors.

It turns out that some fish were leaving the waters during the Devonian and were taking (literally) the first steps on to land. They were at the start of the journey from being fish into becoming amphibians and then reptiles, birds and mammals, including our very own species.

These early terrestrial-exploring vertebrates included *Acanthostega* (a-canth-O STEE-ga), which was 60cm long and had eight digits on its forelimbs, and *Ichthyostega* (ik-THEE-O STEE-ga), which was around 1.5m in length and had seven digits on its hindlimbs. They represent an evolutionary group somewhere between fully aquatic fish and fully terrestrial vertebrates. Both could be found in and around swamps and marshes across the northern hemisphere around 365 million years ago. Both are examples of what scientists call transitional fossils or transitional species, representing a point between one type of organism and another. Here, they show a point in the evolutionary journey from water to land.

During the Devonian, life really began to start moving onto the land. Plants were the first, then insects. Animals that had evolved from fish, such as the *Ichthyostega* (climbing out) and the *Acanthostega* (lurking beneath), were some of the first vertebrates to conquer the land.

The plant life towards the end of the Devonian was different to the flora we think of today. There were no flowers or grass, they evolved much later, but there were some plants we might recognise, because ferns, horsetails and liverworts were present.

And remember the first trees were developing and one of the first and most important (at least in terms of the mass extinction) was the group called *Archaeopteris* (ark-EE op-terr-iss). These looked as though they were a cross between a fern and a palm tree, and they were found around the world. These early trees grew up to around 24m in height and had buds, branches and produced seeds. Importantly, *Archaeopteris* were the first trees to evolve extensive roots.

Behaviour

For many years, scientists thought *Dunkleosteus* was long and thin, looking and acting like a big, armoured eel. However, as more fossils were found, it was discovered that rather than looking like an eel, it is far more likely that

Dunkleosteus acted like one of the open-ocean sharks from today, maybe something like an oceanic whitetip. This discovery, from 2017, meant that the huge prehistoric fish was an active predator, swimming in open waters and also around shallow seas, where it would have actually gone looking for its food, rather than lying in wait.

Its size and shape and the adaptations throughout the skull meant that *Dunkleosteus* was not just a predator but was, what scientists call, an apex predator. This means it would have been at the absolute top of the food chain and was bad news for pretty much every other animal within its ecosystem that was big enough to eat.

We know that its jaws were specially adapted to have immense power and were able to close incredibly quickly. They also created suction, so that when *Dunkleosteus* opened its mouth, it would possibly have drawn prey closer to those deadly slicing plates of bone. Research has shown that these deadly feeding adaptations would have been ideally suited to biting free-swimming prey such as ammonites and many other placoderm fish.

Very often, a palaeontologist wants to understand the behaviour of an extinct animal, but only has fossil bones to go by. Sometimes, though, they are lucky and are given a few more clues. This is what has happened with *Dunkleosteus* and its diet, because there have been lots of fossils found complete with the remains of their meals. Animals such as owls and some snakes regurgitate the parts of their food that are not easily digested and it seems *Dunkleosteus* did the same. These fossilised pellets are full of fish bones, so scientists can even see what its last meal was.

Another thing scientists have noticed is that on many fossils, there are some large grooves along the skull bones, which must have been made by a powerful scraping movement. There is a very short list of suspects which could have caused this sort of injury and palaeontologists believe that not only were they made by another *Dunkleosteus* but that this might also mean they were cannibals and hunted their own kind.

Although the fossilised remains of one *Dunkleosteus* have not yet been found inside the body of another just yet, these scrape marks remain the strongest evidence we have for early cannibalism in these giant predators.

To hunt fast-moving prey with good vision, such as this ammonite, *Dunkleosteus* needed to be speedy and powerful. Here, an unlucky *Gonioclymenia* releases its ink as a defence but it's too late!

GLOSSARY

Acanthostega (a-canth-O STEE-ga)
A transitional species, among the first to move from sea to land.

Algae (al GEE)
A very big group of plants, which do not flower and usually live in aquatic environments. Some algae are tiny and are not attached to anything, but others, such as seaweed, which are the most well-known types of algae, are very big and are attached.

Apex predator
Any predator at the top of a food chain. Sometimes an apex predator will kill and eat other predators. This is also known as hyperpredation.

Archaeopteris (ark-EE op-terr iss)
One of the very first trees to evolve.

Arthropod (AR-throw pod)
An invertebrate which has an exoskeleton where there are segments across the body, and pairs of legs which have joints

in them. Insects, such as ants; arachnids, such as spiders; and crustaceans, such as crabs, are examples of arthropods.

Biodiversity (BI-O DIE-vers it-EE)
The variety of plants, fungi, animals and other groups of organisms within a particular habitat or ecosystem. A healthy habitat or ecosystem will usually have higher levels of biodiversity.

Brachiopod (brak EE-O pod)
This is a large group of soft-bodied marine invertebrates, which live within a two-part shell. Scientists have recorded over 30,000 different fossil species of brachiopod but fewer than 400 species are thought to be alive today. Brachiopods are different to the more commonly seen bivalves today.

Cephalopod (seff a-LO pod)
A group that includes animals such as octopus, squid, cuttlefish and nautilus. The name 'cephalopod' comes from the Greek language and means 'head-foot'. The cephalopods belong to the mollusc group of invertebrates, which also includes slugs, snails, mussels and clams. All cephalopods are marine animals.

Classification
In science, we group things to understand them better and to explore the relationships between these things. Most simply, classifying something in science means to look at the similarities and differences between things to see how they fit a bigger pattern. If you wanted to classify mammals,

you'd look for all the things which help identify a mammal, such as hair and being warm-blooded. If you wanted to classify further, you might separate the bats from the other mammals, based on their differences.

Detritivore (DEE TRY-TI vor)
An organism which mainly eats rotting plant material. Earthworms and dung beetles are examples of detritivores.

Ecological (EE-KO lodge-ik al)
Relating to an organism's ecology, which is the relationship between different organisms and to their physical environment.

Environment (en-vire-on ment)
The 'surroundings' in which an organism, or group of organisms, lives. This includes other species but also weather, climate, mountains, deserts, rivers, lakes, oceans, and so on.

Equator (EE-KWAY tor)
This imaginary line runs around the centre of the Earth and passes through the tropics. It is halfway between the North and South poles and is also known as zero degrees latitude.

Eumerica (YOO mer-rik-aar)
When the super-continent Gondwana began to break up, it formed new land masses. Some of these moved together to form a new giant continent called Eumerica.

Eutrophication (YOO-tro fik-KAY shun)
When too many nutrients and minerals end up in a body of water, such as a lake or river, which then causes too much algae to grow.

Family
There is a whole system used by scientists to categorise or group different species and there are different levels within this system. Within this system, are species, above that there is a genus, and above that the level is called a family.

Geology (JEE-ol O-JEE)
An area of science that studies the Earth, including what it is made from and the processes which made it and continue to shape it.

Greenhouse gas
Like an actual greenhouse, greenhouse gases are able to trap heat. They prevent the trapped heat from escaping through our atmosphere. Carbon dioxide is a greenhouse gas. We need greenhouse gases to keep our planet warm enough for life to exist but if their levels get too high, we start seeing environmental problems through global warming.

Hangenberg (han-genn burg) **event**
This was a spike of extinctions towards the start of the whole Late Devonian mass extinction event.

Ichthyostega (ik-THEE-O STEE-ga)
A transitional species, among the first to move from sea to land.

Kellwasser (kell wass-er) **event**
This was a spike of extinctions at the end of the whole Late Devonian mass extinction event.

Latitude (lat-it UUD)
If you imagine the Earth divided into equally spaced horizontal and vertical lines, the horizontal lines are latitudes. Each line represents a different angle around the planet. The equator is zero degrees, the North Pole is 90 degrees north and South Pole is 90 degrees south.

Laurasia (lorr AY-sha)
When most of the Earth's land formed the supercontinent Pangaea, it was made up mostly of two smaller supercontinents - Gondwana and Laurasia. Laurasia was the more northern of the two that formed part of the Pangaea supercontinent from c. 425 million years ago until it split from Gondwana around 200 million years ago. It finally broke up into smaller continents around 56 million years ago.

Newtons
A unit for measuring force, which is when something changes the movement or motion of an object. It is the force needed to provide a mass of one kilogram with an

acceleration of one metre per second per second. If an object weighs something, then it creates a force which can be measured in newtons. An apple creates about one newton, whereas the average adult human generates a little over 600N.

Niche (NEE-shh)
The match of an organism to a specific environment condition. The ecological niche takes into account food, any possible predators and prey, the habitat, and so on.

Organism (or-gan IZ-mm)
Any living thing. A tree is an organism, so is a shark, and a mushroom. You are an organism.

Palaeoenvironment (pay-LEE-O en-vire-on ment)
Any environment which existed in the prehistoric past.

Palaeontologist (pay-LEE-on tol-O jist)
A very cool type of scientist, who studies dinosaurs, fossils and other extinct forms of life.

Panthalassa (pan-tha lass-a)
The superocean which surrounded the supercontinent Pangaea. At different times, Panthalassa covered 70-85 per cent of the surface of the Earth.

Plankton
Microscopic organisms found in large bodies of fresh or seawater. Plankton can be roughly split into planktonic

plants (called phytoplankton) and planktonic animals (called zooplankton). Plankton forms an essential part of the food chain for millions of other types of organisms.

Supercontinent (SOO-per con-tin-ent)
At times throughout the history of the Earth, all the available land on the planet has been one big mass of land. This is a supercontinent.

Tectonic (tek-ton-ik)
Relating to the structure of the Earth's crust and the processes which occur within it.

Terrestrial (ter-ess TREE-al)
On the land.

Tsunami (SOO nar-ME)
Either one single giant wave, or a series of very large waves, caused by earthquakes or undersea volcanic eruptions.

Collect all eight titles in the EXTINCT series

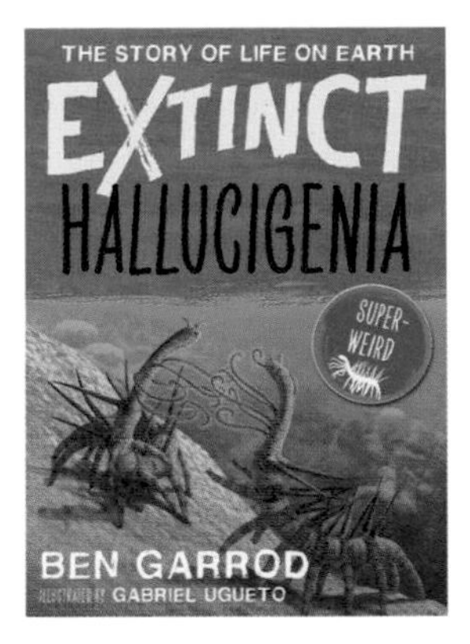

One of the oldest and most mysterious animals ever described, *Hallucigenia* was a kind of sea-living, armoured worm. But it was nothing like the worms we know today. Its body was covered in spines and frills. It had claws at the end of its legs and a mouth lined with sharp teeth.

This strange animal was one of the victims of the End Ordovician mass extinction which claimed 85 per cent of the species living in the world's oceans around 443 million years ago. What could have led to this catastrophe and what caused the appearance of huge glaciers and falling sea levels, leaving many marine ecosystems dry and unable to sustain life at a time when it had only just got started?

Among the first arthropods - animals with jointed legs such as insects and their relatives - trilobites were around on Earth for over 300 million years and survived the first two mass extinctions. There were once at least 20,000 species but all disappeared in the devastating End Permian mass extinction around 252 million years ago.

We'll look at why land animals were affected this time as well as those in the sea. An incredible 96 per cent of marine species went extinct and an almost equally terrible 70 per cent of life on land was wiped out in what is known as the *Great Dying*. This was the closest we've come to losing all life on Earth and the planet was changed forever.

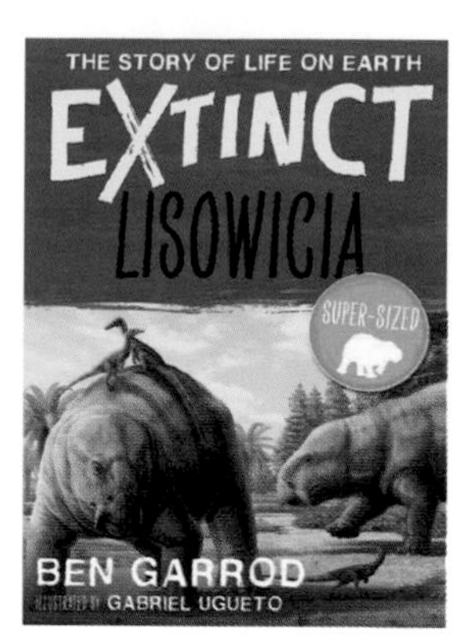

At a massive 9 tonnes, the elephant-sized *Lisowicia* was one of the largest animals on the planet during the Late Triassic. A kind of cross between a mammal and a reptile but not quite either, *Lisowicia* was a distant cousin of the ancient mammals - and they eventually led to our very own ancestors.

We'll discover why the End Triassic mass extinction happened, changing the global environment and making life impossible for around 75 per cent of species. And how, while this fourth mass extinction may have been devastating for most life on Earth, it gave one group of animals - dinosaurs - the chance to dominate the planet for millions of years.

Weighing as much as three adult elephants and as long as a bus, *Tyrannosaurus rex* was one of the mightiest land predators that has ever lived. It had the most powerful bite of any dinosaur and dominated its environment. But not even the biggest dinosaurs were a match for what happened at the end of the Cretaceous, about 66 million years ago.

What happened when an asteroid travelling at almost 40,000km/h crashed into Earth? Creating a shockwave that literally shook the world, its impact threw millions of tonnes of red-hot ash and dust into the atmosphere, blocking out the sun and destroying 75 per cent of life on Earth. Any living thing bigger than a fox was gone and this fifth global mass extinction meant the end of the dinosaurs as we knew them.

A giant marine predator, megalodon grew up to an incredible 18m - longer than three great white sharks, nose to tail. This ferocious monster had the most powerful bite force ever measured. It specialised in killing whales by attacking them from the side, aiming for their heart and lungs.

But, like more than 50 per cent of marine mammals and many others, megalodon disappeared in the End Pliocene mass extinction around 2.5 million years ago. We'll find out why this event affected many of the bigger animals in the marine environment and had an especially bad impact on both warm-blooded animals and predators.

The thylacine, also known as the Tasmanian tiger, is one of a long list of species, ranging from sabre-toothed cats to the dodo, that have been wiped out by humans. The last wild thylacine was shot in 1930 and the last captive thylacine alive died in a zoo in 1936.

We'll explore the mass extinction we are now entering and how we, as a species, have the power to wipe out other species - something no other single species is able to do. Who are the winners and losers and why might it take over seven million years to restore mammal diversity on Earth to what it was before humans arrived?

One of the most endangered animals on our planet, the Hainan gibbon is also one of our closest living relatives. Family groups of these little primates live in the trees on an island off the south coast of China and they feed on leaves and fruit.

But the gibbons are now in serious trouble because of the effects of human population increase around the world and habitat destruction. Without action, this animal might soon be extinct and need a dagger after its name. What can we all do to help stop some of our most interesting, iconic and important species from going extinct?

BEN GARROD is Professor of Evolutionary Biology and Science Engagement at the University of East Anglia. Ben has lived and worked all around the world, alongside chimpanzees in Africa, polar bears in the Arctic and giant dinosaur fossils in South America. He is currently based in the West Country. He broadcasts regularly on TV and radio and is a trustee and ambassador of a number of key conservation organisations. His debut six-book series *So You Think You Know About... Dinosaurs?* and *The Chimpanzee and Me* are also published by Zephyr.

GABRIEL UGUETO is a scientific illustrator, palaeoartist and herpetologist based in Florida. For several years, he was an independent herpetologist researcher and authored papers on new species of neotropical lizards and various taxonomic revisions. As an illustrator, his work reflects the latest scientific hypotheses about the external appearance and the behaviour of the animals, both extinct and extant, that he reconstructs. His illustrations have appeared in books, journals, magazines, museum exhibitions and television documentaries.

Zephyr is an imprint of Head of Zeus.
At Zephyr we are proud to publish books you can read and re-read time and time again because they tell a brilliant story and because they entertain you.

 **@_ZephyrBooks**

 **@_zephyrbooks**

 **HeadofZeusBooks**

readzephyr.com

www.headofzeus.com

ZEPHYR